ADDICTED
to Video Games

Bradley Steffens

ReferencePoint Press®

San Diego, CA

© 2020 ReferencePoint Press, Inc.
Printed in the United States

For more information, contact:
ReferencePoint Press, Inc.
PO Box 27779
San Diego, CA 92198
www.ReferencePointPress.com

LIBRARY OF CONGRESS CATALOGING-IN-PUBLICATION DATA

Names: Steffens, Bradley, author.
Title: Addicted to Video Games/by Bradley Steffens.
Description: San Diego, CA: ReferencePoint Press, Inc., [2020] | Series: Addicted | Audience: Grade 9 to 12. | Includes bibliographical references and index.
Identifiers: Library of Congress Control Number: 2019942214
9781682825761 (eBook) | ISBN 9781682825754 (hardback)
Subjects: LCSH: Video games—Juvenile literature. | video game addiction—Juvenile literature.

Contents

The Newest Addiction

When Vishnu Gopinath was twelve years old, his parents bought him a PlayStation 2 video game console. On the first day Vishnu played for twelve hours. Soon he was spending an average of eight to ten hours a day playing video games. When he did not have school, he played even more—up to fifteen hours a day. Vishnu's favorite games were *God of War*, *Resident Evil 4*, *TimeSplitters*, *Devil May Cry 3*, and *Burnout*. "I'll never forget how good it felt to play for long, long hours," he remembers, "or how easy it was to lose myself in video games completely over time."[1] Eventually, Vishnu's grades began to suffer.

Signs of Addiction

One day Vishnu's mother locked his PlayStation 2 in a cupboard to make sure he spent time studying while she was out of the house. Vishnu became extremely angry. His heart began racing, and he could not think clearly. He was anxious, irritable, and unable to focus. "My hands were shaking, I couldn't think straight," he remembers. "I didn't know this back then, but I was experiencing symptoms that are associated with addiction." When Vishnu finally got his hands on his PlayStation 2, he experienced a profound change of mood. "I plugged it in, and the moment the loading screen came on, I felt all my tension just dissipate," he recalls. "I felt waves and waves of relief wash over me."[2] These feelings, too, were a sign of his growing addiction.

It was not just Vishnu's schoolwork that suffered. He spent so much time gaming that he did not have time for exercise and developed unhealthy eating habits. Already overweight, he became morbidly obese and was diagnosed as prediabetic. His classmates teased him about his weight, pushing him further into isolation. "People made fun of me often, and because of this, it was easy to find my comfort in a video game," he recalls. "A video game wouldn't make fun of me and make me feel bad about my weight. It didn't expect me to be okay with jokes and even outright insults about how I looked. My friends did."[3]

Worried about her son's health and growing isolation, Vishnu's mother repeatedly tried to convince him to cut back on his video game playing, but he would not listen. Finally, she enlisted the help of one of Vishnu's cousins. "I remember this vividly: I was sitting on my couch, playing *TimeSplitters*, and my cousin was sitting with my mother on the sofa on the other side, trying to talk to me about my problem or in their words . . . my 'addiction,'" says Vishnu. His cousin explained to Vishnu that his mother was upset and felt hurt. Vishnu kept his eyes on the screen, not reacting or replying. His cousin said that Vishnu's mother was worried about him. Vishnu did not respond. Vishnu's mother began to cry and told Vishnu's cousin that her son has a problem. "I don't even bother looking up from the TV," Vishnu recalls. "I tell him she's lying." Vishnu's cousin then pointed out the reality of the situation: Vishnu's mother was sitting beside him, crying, and he was playing a video game. Those words broke through. "I couldn't keep denying it anymore," says Vishnu. "All of 13 years old, I hit rock bottom."[4]

Vishnu later developed an addiction to alcohol, so he knows what addiction is. He has no doubt that he was addicted to video gaming. "Every addict knows the feeling," he says. "When you try

> "My hands were shaking, I couldn't think straight. I didn't know this back then, but I was experiencing symptoms that are associated with addiction."[2]
>
> —Vishnu Gopinath, recovering video game addict

and try, and you hate yourself, but then you give in to the thing that controls you."[5]

When a Hobby Becomes an Obsession

The addiction to video games is one of the newest addictions known to medicine. Although software engineers created games to be played on computers as early as 1947, it was only with the advent of home consoles like the Nintendo Entertainment System in the 1980s that video games became part of daily life. But it was the introduction of consoles connected to the Internet, like PlayStation 2 and Xbox Live in the early 2000s, that turned a hobby into an obsession for many gamers. Games like *Grand Theft Auto*, *Call of Duty*, *World of Warcraft*, and *Halo* enabled players in different locations to play both with and against each other in what is known as multiplayer mode. Because these players often are in different time zones, serious gamers may play at odd hours, disrupting their nongaming lives to meet their video game commitments. Real-time, collaborative games increase the risk of video game addiction, because players are not able to simply walk away from the game and resume it at a later time. They keep playing, fearful of missing out on something important.

The introduction of smartphones and other mobile devices extended the reach of video games even further. For example, *Candy Crush Saga* has been downloaded 2.7 billion times since its introduction in 2012, and *Pokémon GO* has been downloaded more than 1 billion times since its debut in 2016. Mobile games allow people to play anywhere at any time—while commuting, waiting in line, on breaks at school and work, and even while watching television.

The World Health Organization (WHO), an agency of the United Nations that is concerned with global public health, estimates that 2.2 billion people play video games regularly, including 150 million in the United States. WHO estimates that 3 percent to 4 percent of gamers worldwide are addicted. That means 77 million people in countries around the world are addicted to video games. At least 5 million are addicted in the United States. Video game addiction is so new that scientists have only begun to look into its causes and its impact on brain functioning, physical health, and social functioning. More research is under way.

Chapter One

What Is Video Game Addiction?

Video game addiction is a behavioral addiction—a mental health condition in which a person repeatedly engages in a certain behavior, even if the behavior causes the person harm. Common behavioral addictions include compulsive gambling, shopping, hoarding, and impulsively stealing things (a condition known as kleptomania). A person with a behavioral addiction often is unable to resist engaging in it; it is a compulsion. Behavioral addictions have serious consequences for the addict. The behavior takes precedence over other life interests and daily activities. As a result it impairs personal, family, social, educational, occupational, and other important areas of functioning. These negative impacts define the addiction.

A Recognized Disorder

In June 2018 the World Health Organization included video game addiction in its *International Classification of Diseases, 11th Revision* (ICD-11). This manual is used by medical professionals around the world to diagnose diseases and mental health conditions. The mental health experts at WHO define video game addiction as "a pattern of gaming behavior ('digital-gaming' or 'video-gaming') characterized by impaired control over gaming, increasing priority given to gaming over other activities to the extent that gaming takes precedence over other interests and daily activities, and continuation or escalation of gaming despite the occurrence of negative consequences."[6]

Video game addiction differs from a healthy enjoyment of gaming when the activity has a negative impact on a person's life and the gamer is unwilling or unable to stop it. To be classified as a disease, the negative impacts must be serious. WHO says,

> For gaming disorder to be diagnosed, the behavior pattern must be of sufficient severity to result in significant impairment in personal, family, social, educational, occupational or other important areas of functioning and would normally have been evident for at least 12 months.[7]

Although video game addicts spend many hours engaged in the activity, it is not the amount of time spent playing that defines video game addiction. A 2014 study by a team of Norwegian researchers found no relation between the amount of time spent gaming and negative outcomes in everyday life. "Video game addiction was related to depression, lower academic achievement, and conduct problems, but time spent on video games was not related to any of the studied negative outcomes,"[8] they write.

The inclusion of the disorder in the WHO manual is important for several reasons. First, it gives medical professionals around the world a single standard for identifying video game addiction. Second, it means that researchers can monitor video game addiction trends and statistics globally, because everyone is defining the disorder the same way, regardless of social, cultural, and medical backgrounds. These statistics will help identify the people who are most at risk of video game addiction. Third, the inclusion of video game addiction in the ICD-11 means more mental health professionals will be able to offer treatment tailored to video game addiction. And fourth, the inclusion of the disorder in the ICD-11 is something that governments will take into account when planning public health strategies and monitoring trends of disorders.

Douglas A. Gentile, a professor of psychology at Iowa State University, is one of those who is pleased by WHO's action. "I think it will help in clinical practice because pediatricians, mental health practitioners and other health care professionals will be alert to symptoms," says Gentile. "There are about 40 million children in the U.S. If 92 percent play video games and 8 percent of them would classify as having gaming disorder, that's over 3 million children in the U.S. today causing serious damage to their lives because of the way they're playing," Gentile explains. "That's a lot of kids who would benefit from getting help but up until now haven't been able to because it hasn't been considered a real diagnosis."[9]

Cam Adair, a recovering video game addict and founder of the online support group Game Quitters, points out that WHO's decision to designate video game addiction as a disorder is also good for healthy gamers. "For too long it's been possible to suggest that someone has a video game addiction based on your own subjective reasoning," says Adair. "No longer. We now have . . . official diagnostic criteria rooted in science and those concerned about someone's gaming can trust a professional assessment."[10]

A Gamer's Struggle with Addiction

An anonymous member of Game Quitters meets all of WHO's criteria for video game addiction. His addiction lasted more than twelve months—several years, in fact—and his relationships and schoolwork suffered. And although he tried to give up video games several times, he always failed. It all began when he was about eight years old and his parents bought him a Nintendo video game console. "That thing got me so excited! I still remember shooting those ducks with a fake gun on the screen!" he says. His parents bought him more games. "I got better at them and then I moved to PlayStation 1. My favorite console ever,"[11] he adds. His favorite games were *Tekken* and *Lara Croft: Tomb Raider*. He also subscribed to *PlayStation: The Official Magazine* to get all the hacks and cheats for his games.

The problem arose when his hobby began to affect his emotions. "I was so competitive!" he recalls. "I was getting so mad when I lost." His parents, however, did not think his passion for gaming was unhealthy. "They thought it was funny," he says. He remembers them saying, "Let the kid be a kid and we go do our adult stuff." But gaming was beginning to replace real life as the most important thing in his life. "Gaming was my escape from the world," he says. "Escape from bullying, from bad family communication, from bad parenting, failed relationships, and psychological issues."[12]

> "Gaming was my escape from the world. Escape from bullying, from bad family communication, from bad parenting, failed relationships, and psychological issues."[12]
>
> —A recovering video game addict at Game Quitters

The teen's hobby became an addiction when the Internet became faster and he began playing *Lineage II*, a massively multiplayer online role-playing game (MMORPG) in which he was part

Like gambling addiction, video game addiction is a behavioral addiction. A person with a behavioral addiction is often unable to resist engaging in that behavior, even when the behavior causes them harm.

of a worldwide team. "My character was my life," he admits. "I remember I used to daydream about the game during school time. Draw pictures of weapons and enemies! Making phone calls with my guild clan members. I even had my own guild." When he was seventeen, he played for twenty-four hours straight just to move

Warning Signs of Video Game Addiction

A Forever Recovery is an addiction treatment center that offers help to video game addicts. It provides a list of characteristics that, when taken together, could mean that a person's gaming hobby is becoming a problem. Among students, failing to complete assignments, sleepiness during the day, a loss of interest in school activities, and declining grades are associated with unhealthy levels of gaming. Other warning signs include:

- Playing in secret, or lying to family members, friends, or others about time spent playing or extent of involvement with the game
- Isolating from family and friends to play video games
- Using games to escape from reality, or to relieve feelings of hopelessness, anxiety, or depression
- Showing signs of anxiety or depression
- Alienating from/deteriorating relationships with friends and family
- Becoming restless, moody, irritable, or depressed when unable to game
- Suffering from sleep disturbance and/or fatigue
- Losing interest in other activities and hobbies, and real-life relationships
- Increasingly ignoring personal hygiene
- Eating irregularities such as skipping meals
- Changes in weight (noticeable loss or gain)
- Migraines caused by intense concentration or eye strain
- Carpal tunnel syndrome from the repetitive use of gaming device or mouse

A Forever Recovery, "Video Game Addiction Facts." https://aforeverrecovery.com.

up one level of the game. "My psychology started to change, I became more bored of real life, more avoidant of people, and sports started to get less interesting and more tiring. I became less fit and more fat. I had bad eating and sleeping habits, and poor posture." He began to have problems with his schoolwork, and his parents pressured him to stop playing video games. "Those were really bad times, but that game was my life," he remembers. "I was very respected and liked online. That was tremendous to me because in real life I was getting bullied and mistreated a lot, and thus had very low self-esteem."[13]

He went to college to study computer science, thinking he would become a game designer and give others the joy that gaming gave him. But his studies suffered because of his gaming. It took him seven years to complete a degree that most of his classmates completed in four years. The addicted gamer finally recognized that he had a problem. At twenty-five he began to cut back on MMORPGs, but he still played *World of Warcraft*, *League of Legends*, and *Hearthstone*. He finally broke his addiction at age twenty-nine. "I still have self-esteem issues that I am working on," he says. "My family and I are working to fix our issues after all these years. I am inexperienced with relationships and still a virgin. I moved back in with my parents at 25 and still live with them at 30. I feel kind of stuck, but at the same time I am trying to move forward little by little."[14]

The Demographics of Video Game Addiction

The anonymous Game Quitters contributor fits the demographic profile of a video game addict. Demographics are statistical data relating to the population and particular groups within it. Public health officials use this data to identify the groups most at risk of a disease or mental condition. In the case of video gaming, the Pew Research Center has found that 43 percent of US adults play video games on a computer, TV, game console, or portable device like a cell phone, but those under fifty years old are twice

as likely to play video games as those who are older. Fully 55 percent of people under the age of fifty play video games sometimes or often, while only 28 percent of those fifty and over do. As the age goes down, the number of people who play video games— and are at risk of becoming addicted to video games—goes up. Among US adults aged eighteen to thirty-four, 60 percent play video games. The activity is even more popular among teens. An incredible 90 percent of US teens say they play video games.

While large numbers of both men and women play video games, men play more than women do, according to the Pew Research Center. Among all ages, 47 percent of men play video games, compared with 39 percent of women. The gender difference is greater among younger adults: 72 percent of men ages eighteen to twenty-nine play video games compared with 49 percent of women in the same age range. The gender gap is smaller among teens. An astounding 97 percent of teenage boys play video games, but 83 percent of girls do, too. There is an important difference between the genders, however. Far more young men (33 percent) identify themselves as "gamers" than do young women (9 percent). Identifying oneself as a gamer reveals a deep connection to the video game world. This connection shows up in the number of people actually addicted to video games. According to Tech Addiction, a Canadian treatment center and information service for people who struggle with controlling their use of technology, 94 percent of gaming addicts are male. The average age of a gaming addict is twenty-four years old.

José Antonio Hita Ruiz is another gamer who fits the risk profile. His father was an alcoholic, and his mother supported the family by working long hours. Ruiz comforted himself by playing video games. His grades suffered, and he was bullied, so he soon dropped out of school. He filled his time by playing video games. "I wasn't even playing with other people; it was just me and the same few games, again and again," Ruiz recalls. "Some people may misinterpret if I say 'like a drug.' But in my experience, it was like a drug." His friends went off to college, leaving Ruiz behind. "There was a point where I was completely alone,"[15] he says. Ruiz became depressed and began to have suicidal thoughts. To numb the pain, he played video games even more. Finally, he had an emotional breakdown and checked himself into a hospital. He knew he had to quit gaming or else he would end his life. He never played again.

> "I wasn't even playing with other people; it was just me and the same few games, again and again. Some people may misinterpret if I say 'like a drug.' But in my experience, it was like a drug."[15]
>
> —José Antonio Hita Ruiz, recovering video game addict

How Teens View Time Spent Playing Video Games

A 2018 Pew Research Center survey found that 41 percent of teenage boys think they spend too much time playing video games. Among teenage girls, only 11 percent said they play video games too much. Overall, 26 percent of teens believe they play video games too much, while 22 percent believe they play too little.

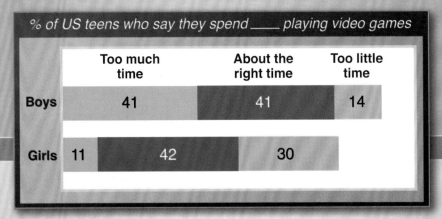

41% of teenage boys say they spend too much time playing video games

% of US teens who say they spend _____ playing video games

	Too much time	About the right time	Too little time
Boys	41	41	14
Girls	11	42	30

Note: Respondents who do not play video games are not shown.

Source: Andrew Perrin, "5 Facts About Americans and Video Games," Pew Research Center, September 17, 2018. www.pewresearch.org.

The Prevalence of Video Game Addiction

Experts disagree about how many people are addicted to video games. WHO estimates that between 3 percent and 4 percent of all gamers meet its criteria for addiction. That would mean that between 4.5 million and 6 million Americans are video game addicts. Researchers led by Andrew Przybylski, a professor and experimental psychologist at the Oxford Internet Institute, a part of Oxford University in England, however, believe the number is much smaller.

In a 2018 study Przybylski's team analyzed surveys of 18,932 gamers in the United States, Canada, the United Kingdom, and Germany who played online video games. To measure addictiveness, the team used the American Psychiatric Association's definition of Internet gaming disorder (IGD), which is slightly different from the World Health Organization's definition of gaming disorder. Przybylski's team found that while a third of gamers reported having some of the symptoms of addiction, only 0.3 percent to 1 percent of gamers reported having all of them and thus qualifying as addicts. If correct, Przybylski's estimate would

Video Game Addiction Defined

In June 2018 the World Health Organization recognized video game addiction as a mental health disorder. The organization's *International Classification of Diseases, 11th Revision* (ICD-11) provides a definition of the condition:

> Gaming disorder is characterized by a pattern of persistent or recurrent gaming behaviour ('digital gaming' or 'video-gaming'), which may be online (i.e., over the Internet) or offline, manifested by:
>
> 1. impaired control over gaming (e.g., onset, frequency, intensity, duration, termination, context);
> 2. increasing priority given to gaming to the extent that gaming takes precedence over other life interests and daily activities; and
> 3. continuation or escalation of gaming despite the occurrence of negative consequences. The behaviour pattern is of sufficient severity to result in significant impairment in personal, family, social, educational, occupational or other important areas of functioning.
>
> The pattern of gaming behaviour may be continuous or episodic and recurrent. The gaming behaviour and other features are normally evident over a period of at least 12 months in order for a diagnosis to be assigned, although the required duration may be shortened if all diagnostic requirements are met and symptoms are severe.

World Health Organization, "6C51 Gaming Disorder," ICD-11 for Mortality and Morbidity Statistics, April 2019. https://icd.who.int.

mean that between 450,000 to 1.5 million Americans are addicted to Internet video games. "Video game addiction might be a real thing, but it is not the epidemic that some have made it out to be,"[16] wrote the authors of an editorial that appeared along with the study in the *Journal of American Psychiatry*.

Not everyone agrees with Przybylski's findings. A 2017 study led by Gentile used a definition developed by the IGD Working Group of the National Academy of Sciences to identify video game addiction—a definition that covers both online and offline gaming. "Despite its name, IGD does not require that individuals exhibit symptoms of addiction solely with online video games," explains Gentile's team. "Problematic use can occur in both offline and online settings."[17] Gentile's team found that between 1 percent and 9 percent of gamers are addicted to video games. According to this finding, between 1.5 million and 13.5 million Americans are suffering from video game addiction. That means as much as 4 percent of the US population could be addicted to video games. "This is a serious thing," says Adair. "We need to help people with it. It's not enough to continue to ignore it."[18]

Mental health experts disagree on how widespread video game addiction is, but there is no doubt that it exists. And it is having devastating effects on millions of gamers.

Chapter Two

Why Are Video Games So Addictive?

More than 2 billion people around the world play video games without becoming addicted. For some it is an idle pastime, a way to alleviate boredom when there is nothing else to do. For others it is a passion that fills their life with exciting challenges and momentous achievements. Whatever the reason for playing, the vast majority of gamers are able to keep their game play in the realm of entertainment and amusement. Others are not. "You let it go from being a passion to an obsession," says Douglas A. Gentile. "You let it go from being something you enjoy to something that's controlling you."[19] Researchers are investigating why this happens to some gamers but not to others. As with other behavioral addictions, there seem to be many contributing factors to the addiction.

To better understand why people become addicted to video games, researchers at National Kaohsiung University of Hospitality and Tourism in Taiwan looked at the different reasons people have for playing video games. They found that video games provide most players with a sense of satisfaction in their accomplishments. Nonaddicted gamers play to experience this satisfaction. Addicted gamers, by contrast, do not experience this kind of satisfaction. They are motivated to play by dissatisfaction, which arises from the absence of game playing. Addicted gamers play video games as a relief from dissatisfaction, rather than in the pursuit of satisfaction.

The Chemical Basis of Fun

Both addicted and nonaddicted gamers are motivated to play by sensations originating from chemical processes in the brain. One of the ways that mammals—including human beings—learn to survive is through a chemical reward system that exists in the brain. When a person does something that will help ensure survival—such as eating, drinking, or solving a problem—the brain releases a chemical known as dopamine as a reward. Dopamine is one of about twenty chemicals in the brain known as neurotransmitters. These chemicals allow nerve cells, or neurons, to transmit chemical messages to one another. The release of dopamine creates a sensation of pleasure in the brain, which reinforces the behavior that released it.

Dopamine can be released by the successful completion of activities not related to survival. For example, completing a task, solving a problem, and overcoming a challenge in a video game can also release dopamine, creating pleasurable sensations that make the game fun. For most gamers these sensations provide a pleasant escape from everyday life. But addicted gamers use video games to modify their moods, much as a person might use alcohol or drugs to alter his or her mental state.

Dopamine is only released when a successful outcome follows a period of uncertainty, as when an animal follows an unknown scent to a reward of food. Dopamine reinforces the value of the survival-enhancing action. However, if there is no uncertainty, there is no reward. For example, correctly adding two plus two does not trigger a reward, because the outcome of the challenge is certain. Video games have an element of uncertainty built in; the player does not know beforehand whether he or she will succeed in the game.

To release dopamine, the brain also must realize it has succeeded at what it was attempting to do. Performing a task with an unclear outcome does not release dopamine. In nature, success is known by finding food or catching prey. In video games, success is marked by accumulating points, solving a puzzle, or completing a level, for instance. This is known as incremental goal progress. As a player reaches these incremental goals, the brain rewards the behavior with dopamine. These surges of dopamine keep the player motivated to meet ever-more difficult challenges.

To keep people playing and buying their games, video game designers make sure that their games are difficult enough to create uncertainty, but easy enough to achieve incremental goals. "Games give you a feedback loop," says Cam Adair. "You get to see growth and progress, and it happens immediately through instant gratification."[20]

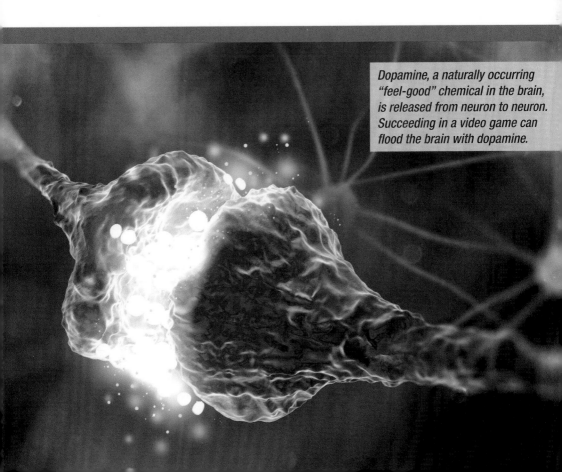

Dopamine, a naturally occurring "feel-good" chemical in the brain, is released from neuron to neuron. Succeeding in a video game can flood the brain with dopamine.

Addicted to *Candy Crush Saga*

A thirty-four-year-old woman in Fleetwood, England, found the go-anywhere availability of mobile video games to be irresistible. Natasha Woolsley says she played *Candy Crush Saga* on her cell phone up to eighteen hours a day, neglecting her son, Taylor, and running up credit card debt. She explains:

> I honestly can't remember a gap between starting and playing every waking moment, sometimes up to 18 hours a day. Because it was on my phone, I could play on the school run, in the bath, even on the toilet. I became so obsessed I'd wake in the middle of the night wanting more, and hide in the bathroom to play for another few hours so I could move up one level. I was completely out of control. . . .
>
> I'd regularly lose track of time and forget to pick Taylor up from school so [I] would get a call asking where I was. I stopped reading to him at bedtime and I'd just throw a packet of crisps and a chocolate bar in his school lunchbox because I didn't have the time or energy to make anything healthy. Even when I was with him I wasn't "there". I was wanting to get my phone out, like an alcoholic thinking about their next drink. . . .

Quoted in Matthew Barbour, "Mum Addicted to Candy Crush Played 18 Hours a Day Losing Her Boyfriend, Her Job and Thousands of Pounds," *Daily Mirror* (London), January 13, 2018. www.mirror.co.uk.

Game designers also use a technique known as variable ratio reinforcement schedules to sustain interest in their games. They do this by creating small digital prizes or awards that the gamer collects while playing. The location of these prizes, their frequency, and their value are all unknown to the player. Some may be large, others may be small. The anticipation of earning the reward keeps the players engaged and makes it hard for them to stop playing. It is the same technique that slot machine designers use to keep gamblers playing. The gambler never knows if the next pull of the lever is going to yield nothing, a small reward, or a jackpot. This uncertainty, and the occasional, or variable, winning of a reward, keeps the dopamine flowing and the gambler playing.

The Lure of Loot Boxes

Variable ratio reinforcement schedules are also used to govern the contents of digital containers known as loot boxes. Found in popular video games, including *Overwatch*, *Star Wars: Battlefront II*, *Counter-Strike*, *FIFA Ultimate Team*, and *Fortnite*, loot boxes contain a random assortment of virtual items (loot) to help a player advance in a video game or customize a player's avatar, or online character. Players purchase loot boxes for anywhere from one dollar to three hundred dollars or more in real-world money. Using the principle of variable ratio reinforcement schedules, the contents of the loot boxes are not known until the player pays for them. Often the item cannot be won inside the game; it can only be obtained by opening a loot box. Because these items can be extremely desirable, and because players spend real money on them, the stakes for winning them are high. Not surprisingly, the anticipation of winning desired loot creates a chemical reaction in the brain that is similar to the one that is triggered by gambling. Loot boxes are another video game feature that feed into video game addiction.

Scientific researchers have found similarities between buying loot boxes and problem gambling. A 2018 survey of 7,422 video game players asked about their video game playing and gambling habits. The researchers found that 78 percent of the participants had bought a loot box in a video game, and 87 percent had bought an item other than a loot box in a video game. There were differences between those who bought loot boxes and those who only bought other items. There were also differences between those who spent small amounts of money on loot boxes and those who spent large amounts. "This study shows a relationship between loot box spending and problem gambling," the researchers write.

> This link was stronger than a link between problem gambling and buying other in-game items with real-world money, suggesting that the gambling-like features of loot boxes are specifically responsible for the observed relationship between problem gambling and spending on loot boxes.[21]

One video game player who is hooked on loot boxes calls herself CadenceLikesVGs. Her game of choice is *Path of Exile (PoE)*, an online role-playing game. *PoE* offers loot boxes to let the players customize their character's gear about every three months. Each loot box costs around three dollars to open, but the contents are governed by variable ratio reinforcement schedules. As a result a player might get the desired item on the first purchase, but it usually takes several attempts before the item is obtained.

Players like Cadence can get swept up in the effort to get the items they want. "When your brain works like mine, you can't stop," she says. "There is always the little voice [in] the back of your head that goes, 'Yeah no man, you should've quit like 30 boxes ago,' but even when you're telling yourself to stop, you're still clicking buy, and you're still opening boxes." Cadence says the least she ever spent to complete a gear set was $140 and the most was $400. "People tend to jump on the lootboxes thinking they'll get a deal, but that's not how gambling works," Cadence says. "The house always wins."[22]

> "When your brain works like mine, you can't stop. . . . Even when you're telling yourself to stop, you're still clicking buy, and you're still opening boxes."[22]
>
> —CadenceLikesVGs, a gamer who is hooked on buying loot boxes

Loot boxes are big business, with about $30 billion in sales each year, according to the technology consultancy firm Juniper Research. Analysts estimate that the popular game *Fortnite*, which is free to download, earns $300 million a month in loot box sales. The items in *Fortnite* loot boxes are purely for show, containing new costumes, items, and dance moves for players' avatars. They do not help the player advance in the game, but they impress other gamers and are considered prestigious.

The video game industry disputes the charge that loot boxes are addictive or a form of gambling. "Loot boxes are a voluntary feature in certain video games that provide players with another way to obtain virtual items that can be used to enhance their in-game experiences. They are not gambling," states the Entertainment Software Association, the video game industry's trade association.

Depending on the game design, some loot boxes are earned and others can be purchased. In some games, they have elements that help a player progress through the video game. In others, they are optional features and are not required to progress or succeed in the game. In both cases, the gamer makes the decision.[23]

Government Officials Investigate Loot Boxes

Loot boxes have many things in common with games of chance. The loot box buyer spends real money to open a virtual container without knowing ahead of time what it contains. While the gamer always receives something in the loot box, it may take several plays before he or she obtains a desired item. The most desired loot box items appear randomly, just as winning combinations in a slot machine do. The similarity to slot machines is so strong that in 2018 Belgium and the Netherlands banned loot boxes, ruling that they constitute gambling.

Australia and the United States are also looking at regulating their use. In a letter to the Entertainment Software Rating Board, a software industry self-regulatory organization, Senator Maggie Hassan of New Hampshire wrote: "The prevalence of in-game micro-transactions, often referred to as 'loot boxes,' raises several concerns surrounding the use of psychological principles and enticing mechanics that closely mirror those often found in casinos and games of chance." Under pressure from Hassan and others, the Federal Trade Commission was scheduled to hold a public workshop in August 2019 to examine consumer protection issues related to video game loot boxes.

Quoted in Benjamin Pu, "What Are Loot Boxes? FTC Will Investigate $30B Video Game Industry," NBC News, November 28, 2018. www.nbcnews.com.

Hardwired for Addiction

The bright lights and the lure of hidden treasure excite the curiosity of most video game players, but the brains of some players appear to be structured in a way that makes them more receptive to the stimulation and less able to walk away from it. Researchers at the University of Nottingham in the United Kingdom have found that the brain circuitry of video game addicts is similar to the circuitry of people with drug addictions. In 2018 the Nottingham researchers compared brain imaging of people with video game addiction to that of people who are not addicted. Healthy nonaddicted individuals, known as controls, provide a standard for measurement. The researchers found that compared to the controls, video game addicts have impaired functioning of the prefrontal cortex, the part of the brain responsible for coordinating and adjusting complex behavior, focusing and organizing attention, and impulse control. As a result video game addicts have poorer cognitive control, working memory, decision-making capabilities, and regulation of their emotions. They find it hard to break away from their video games and return to their daily lives.

The prefrontal cortex is also the area of the brain that gives rise to attention-deficit/hyperactivity disorder (ADHD), a mental condition associated with a lack of impulse control. Because they lack impulse control, people with ADHD are particularly susceptible to video game addiction. A 2017 study by scientists at Kaohsiung Medical University in Kaohsiung City, Taiwan, found that 39 percent of young adults with IGD also met the diagnostic criteria for ADHD. "The results suggested that IGD is associated with ADHD among young adults and that young adults with both IGD and ADHD have higher impulsivity and hostility,"[24] they write.

The University of Nottingham researchers believe another part of the brain also contributes to video game addiction. They found that video game addicts have a deficiency in their brain's reward system—the system that releases dopamine and other reward

26

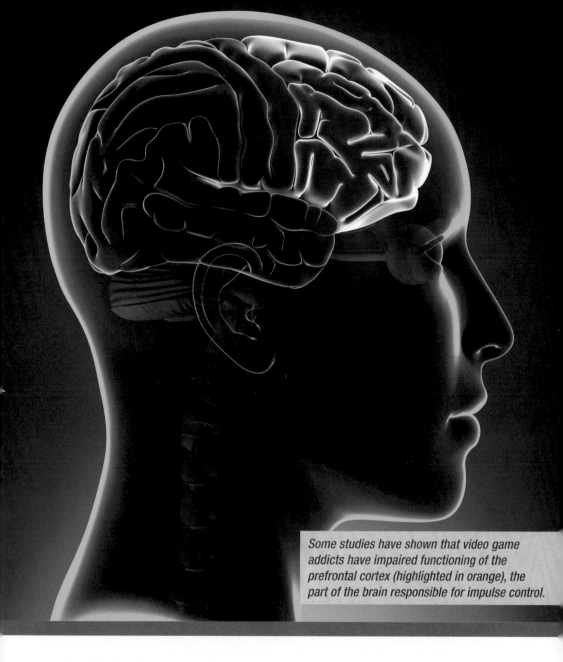

Some studies have shown that video game addicts have impaired functioning of the prefrontal cortex (highlighted in orange), the part of the brain responsible for impulse control.

chemicals. This deficiency means that it takes more video game play, greater risks, and bigger rewards to release the dopamine the players crave. This deficiency is similar to those found in individuals with substance-related addictions. "This suggests both substance-related addictions and behavioral addictions share common predisposing factors and may be part of an addiction syndrome,"[25] write the researchers.

Parenting and Video Game Addiction

Many people, especially those associated with the video game industry, blame video game addiction on parenting practices. They say that video game addiction occurs among children and adolescents because parents fail to set limits for video game playing. For example, in November 2018, the news outlet Bloomberg released a video entitled *"Fortnite" Addiction Is Forcing Kids into Video-Game Rehab*, referring to problems associated with the popular game *Fortnite*. The best-known player of *Fortnite*, a gamer called Ninja, who has more than 4 million followers on Twitter, tweeted: "Title should be 'Terrible parents don't know how to take their kids gaming system away.'"[26]

The majority of video game addicts are not children. Most addicts are adults between the ages of eighteen and twenty-four.

However, the data does not support the blame-the-parents argument. First, many children become addicted to video games because of underlying conditions such as ADHD or impaired brain functioning—things parents and guardians do not have control over. Second, addicted gamers often hide their problem from family members, just as substance abusers do. Third, the vast majority of video game addicts are not children. "Most gaming addicts are young adults, 18 to 24, who develop the problem after they no longer have parental supervision," notes Adair. "Certainly, parents need to set boundaries and do all of that, but it's far more complex than just 'it's a parenting problem.'"[27]

Some video game addicts are hardwired for addiction, having impaired brain circuitry that contributes to their behavior. Others come from a home with an absent parent or one struggling with addiction, leaving a young gamer to develop habits that morph into addiction. Many have no underlying mental or parental problem but are bullied or teased by their peers and retreat into a virtual world where they are known and liked. The rest are otherwise healthy but are manipulated by game features that are intentionally designed to trigger the release of the pleasure-giving chemical dopamine at regular intervals. This is similar to how cigarettes release the addictive drug nicotine—a fact that the video game industry refuses to acknowledge. "Big gaming is like the new tobacco industry in the way that they're approaching this," asserts Adair. "They've been in complete denial."[28] Without warnings about addiction, without age limits for certain games, and without widespread awareness that video game addiction even exists, millions of gamers never have a chance against the unseen forces arrayed against them.

> "Certainly, parents need to set boundaries and do all of that, but it's far more complex than just 'it's a parenting problem.'"[27]
>
> —Cam Adair, founder of Game Quitters, an online support group for video game addicts

Chapter Three

How Do People Become Addicted to Video Games?

Each addict's pathway to addiction is unique, but many addiction stories have common themes. This is especially true of video game addiction stories, because nearly all video game players first encounter the technology in childhood. Exposure to the dopamine-producing features of video games can be especially dangerous to children, because they have no experience with mood-altering substances and no knowledge about how to moderate their use. They are wide open to the manipulation of their brain chemicals. "No matter what you insert as something people want to use, whether it be video games or methamphetamines or crack cocaine, it's going to hit the brain in a similar fashion," says Canadian addiction counselor Elizabeth Loudon. "The people that develop video games understand that. They understand what the brain is looking for, and how to hook a young person to get that dopamine rush over and over again, and so it hooks them into wanting to play continuously."[29]

For children with underlying brain development problems, the effects of a video game's dopamine rush can be overwhelming. "To a twelve-year-old with ADHD, getting a PlayStation was like crack," says recovering video game addict Vishnu Gopinath. "Except this had flashing lights and colorful characters, and didn't kill your dreams and ruin your life."[30] Gopinath's reaction to video games is not uncommon. A 2017 study by researchers at Iowa State University found that up to 9 percent of US youth ages eight to eighteen meet the criteria for video game addiction.

An Escape from Reality

For some youths, the dopamine rush provided by video games is pleasant, but what matters even more to them is the safety and security of the alternate universe they enter when they play video games. This is often the case for young people who are bullied at school or simply social outcasts. Game Quitters founder Cam Adair says that when he was in eighth grade, older students would chase him down and try to stuff him into a trash can in the schoolyard—a game they called "Can we put Cam in a garbage can?" His teammates on his hockey team bullied him as well. "After a game . . . , we all got on the team bus to head back home, and for an entire hour I laid at the back of the team bus in fetal position being spit on," Adair remembers. To avoid the bullies, Adair began to skip school. "The less I went to school and the less I went to hockey, the more I played video games," he says. "They were a place for me to escape to, a place I had more control over my experience."[31] The use of games to escape or relieve a negative mood is one of the nine diagnostic criteria for video game addiction, as determined by the American Psychiatric Association (APA).

Adair dropped out of high school and began to play video games up to sixteen hours a day. Spending large amounts of time playing video games is another step toward addiction. The APA's *Diagnostic and Statistical Manual of Mental Disorders, Fifth Edition* states that a persistent

"To a twelve-year-old with ADHD, getting a PlayStation was like crack."[30]

—Vishnu Gopinath, recovering video game addict

"The less I went to school and the less I went to hockey, the more I played video games. They were a place for me to escape to, a place I had more control over my experience."[31]

—Cam Adair, recovering video game addict and founder of Game Quitters and recurrent participation in computer gaming for typically eight to ten hours or more per day and at least thirty hours per week is an essential feature of video game addiction.

Adair's parents did not just allow him to stay home from school and play video games. They said that if he was going to drop out of school, he needed to get a job—which he did. He actually got a series of them, but it was only for show. He explains:

> Every morning my dad would drop me off at a restaurant where I was a prep cook. As soon as he drove off I would walk across the street and catch the bus back home, sneaking in through my window and going to sleep—I had been up all night playing video games. A few weeks later my parents would wonder about a paycheck, so I would make up an excuse that I quit or I got fired or whatever else I could confuse them with. Then I would "get another job," rinse and repeat.[32]

Adair's deceptive behavior fulfilled two more of the APA's diagnostic criteria for Internet gaming disorder: deceiving family members, therapists, or others regarding the amount of gaming and jeopardizing or losing a significant relationship, job, or educational or career opportunity because of participation in games. Lying about one's game playing is another marker on the road to addiction.

Adair had in fact met several more of the APA's diagnostic criteria for video game addiction. He had lost interest in real-life relationships and previous hobbies as a result of his video gaming. He had tried to quit playing but failed. He experienced withdrawal symptoms, including anxiety and sadness, when he could not play. Worst of all, he continued to play despite being aware that he had psychological and social problems. "When I was gaming I didn't have to think about how bad my life had gotten, and how depressed I was," he writes. "Unfortunately, although I could

Whether a person is playing video games or taking drugs like methamphetamines (shown), the brain is stimulated in a similar fashion. Both create a dopamine rush that can be especially dangerous to children.

escape from dealing with it, games didn't fix the problem, and things only continued to get worse, until one night when I wrote a suicide note." As he thought about taking his life, Adair at last realized he had a problem. "I no longer felt safe with myself," he remembers. "So I asked my dad if he could help me and I started to see a counselor."[33] After receiving treatment, Adair decided to end his video gaming rather than end his life.

The Risks of Multiplayer Games

While some people play video games as an escape from people, others view gaming as a way to connect to others. "Gaming is a sense of community," says Adair. "It's where you feel welcome and safe. It's where you feel accepted."[34] Multiplayer games like

A Dangerous Obsession

Like 125 million other gamers worldwide, seventeen-year-old Carl Thompson of Preston, England, played *Fortnite*, a multiplayer video game that involves building virtual fortifications and battling foes. Thompson describes how *Fortnite* became an obsession that led him to skip his college classes, steal money from his parents, begin using drugs, and attempt to take his own life.

> All I cared about was *Fortnite*. It's almost impossible to describe how quickly it happened, the bubble I was in, how my old life felt like a dream.
>
> The more battles you win, the more you want to keep playing. Each time you're killed you're automatically dropped back into the battle zone, so it's like being on an endless loop, and all you want is to move up the rankings for more rewards and better status.
>
> I was doing all-nighters three or four nights a week. When I hadn't slept, I'd just take more speed [amphetamines] and carry on. I was a complete state, miserable and unable to function . . . kept up by the speed and not eating.
>
> I just had to escape this existence, and the only way I knew how was to kill myself. I climbed out of my bedroom window and looked down, wanting to end it all.

Thompson's father heard the window open and pulled his son to safety. Thompson received counseling and now speaks out against video game addiction.

Quoted in Rhian Lubin and Matthew Barbour, "'Fortnite Made Me a Suicidal Drug Addict': Dad Saves Son, 17, from Death Plunge After He Gets Hooked on Video Game," *Daily Mirror* (London), July 31, 2018. www.mirror.co.uk.

Fortnite, League of Legends, Dota 2, Apex Legends, Team Fortress 2, Overwatch, and *Counter-Strike: Global Offensive* enable gamers to team up with other players and communicate as they play. A player's teammates could be anywhere in the world. As they advance on a quest, they often form a bond. These bonds can grow into friendships with the gamers making plans to play together at certain times, sharing gaming tips and secrets, and even discussing details about their lives.

Such friendships are generally positive, but they can also feed into an addiction. A gamer can feel pressure to play with online friends at the appointed times, putting gaming commitments ahead of real-life commitments like attending classes or going to work. A gamer can also feel pressure to not leave a multiplayer game in progress, because they do not want to disappoint their online friends and contribute to their team's defeat. "My game of choice was Counter-Strike," says a recovering video game addict in the United Kingdom. "To me, it was my everything. The team-player element of it was incredibly powerful as a way of persuading you to not want to stop playing, because the worry of letting your 'teammates' down was so strong."[35]

Such intense gaming can be harmless, but for some it is another step on the pathway to addiction. This is especially true when the gaming produces anxiety, rather than pleasure. The APA defines video game addiction as the persistent and recurrent use of the Internet to engage in games, often with other players, leading to clinically significant impairment or distress. A gamer who goes by the online name of Slitz_Treaver began to realize that he was addicted to video games when he started playing the multiplayer game *Overwatch* and found that it produced anxiety rather than pleasure in his life. "Initially I was really enjoying the game, reliving the fun moments in multiplayer gaming," he says. "However, as Overwatch is an online multiplayer game which is heavily dependent on teammates' performance, its nature slowly drew the toxicity inside me. I would get frustrated and often blamed strangers on our team. I tried really hard to not blame my friends, accept criticism and feedbacks from them, although sometimes the toxicity still got me."[36]

Pressure from online friends and playing partners can encourage people to do things they otherwise might not do, including using drugs to enhance performance during round-the-clock gaming sessions. "I was exhausted doing all-nighters, so my mates said I should try playing with amphetamines," admits Carl Thompson, a gamer in Preston, England, who says he was addicted to the multiplayer game *Fortnite*. "I've always been anti-drugs, but all I wanted to do was play the game more, and this seemed the only way."[37]

The use of drugs to continue playing or enhance the experience is common. A 2018 study by researchers in the Czech Republic found that more than 75 percent of gamers use some drug while gaming. The vast majority use legal drugs, including caffeine, tobacco, and alcohol. Smaller numbers use illegal drugs, including amphetamines and cocaine. More than 40 percent of gamers said that their reasons for taking drugs were game-related. Some of the reasons gamers use drugs include to avoid sleep (25.8 percent), increase concentration (15.6 percent), manage tension (7.3 percent), increase courage (4.1 percent), avoid hunger (2.7 percent), and manage insomnia (2.0 percent).

> "I've always been anti-drugs, but all I wanted to do was play the game more, and [using drugs] seemed the only way."[37]
>
> —Carl Thompson, recovering video game addict

Struggling to Quit

Pressure from gaming peers can also make it more difficult for gamers to cut back on or stop their playing. According to the APA, the inability to control or reduce participation in games is another symptom of video game addiction. Adair recounts how he quit abruptly and completely—a method known as cold turkey—and did not play a video game for two years. However, one day he and

A young man plays the web-based game Fortnite. *Multiplayer games like* Fortnite *enable gamers to team up with other players around the world and communicate as they play.*

a new roommate, Ben, were discussing video games and realized that they used to play the same game—*StarCraft*. Ben challenged Adair to play, but Adair, knowing he was a video game addict, refused to play. "I told him I had quit, and really didn't want to play video games anymore," remembers Adair. "He just laughed it off." Ben persisted in his challenges, and Adair finally gave in. He lost badly, and his pride was hurt. "Humiliated in defeat, I committed to doing everything possible to improve so he could never beat me like that again, and for the next 5 months I played 16 hours a day, and did nothing else but game."[38] After being game-free for two years, he had relapsed.

The struggle to quit is a common one. Another anonymous gamer at Game Quitters says that he had a problem playing games that never end, such as *Team Fortress 2*, *Minecraft*, and *World of Warcraft*. He estimates that he logged more than four thousand hours gaming. "Realizing this destroyed me. Gaming has worsened my academics significantly, forcing me to retake

A Tech Worker Struggles to Abstain from Video Games

"I'm like an alcoholic working at a bar," says a twenty-seven-year-old recovering video game addict who works for a Seattle company that performs maintenance on cloud servers, clusters of computers connected to the Internet. Because he works with technology all day, he constantly feels tempted to return to his video game habit.

His interest in video games began early. As a toddler, he sat on his father's lap as they played simple video games on a Mac Classic II computer. When he was in elementary school, his parents bought him a Super Nintendo video game system. He spent countless hours playing *Yoshi's Story*, a game where the main character collected "lucky fruit."

When he was eleven, his parents split up, leaving him with more time to play video games unsupervised. He did not realize it at the time, but he had begun to use video games to soothe his emotional pain. As a teenager, he became interested in music and acting, but playing video games offered him an escape from his emotional difficulties. "[I'd] go online instead of dealing with my feelings," he says.

The young man attended college out of state, which gave him more freedom. He spent more and more time playing video games, and his grades suffered. Unable to keep up with the demands of an engineering major, he switched to business. After graduating in 2016, he moved home. Realizing he had a technology addiction, he began to attend twelve-step meetings, starting his recovery.

Quoted in Associated Press, "'Tech Addicts' Seek Solace in 12 Steps and Rehab," *Tampa Bay Times* (St. Petersburg, FL), December 26, 2018. www.tampabay.com.

a year," he says. "I had social anxiety, and my brain felt jacked on something." He tried to quit, but failed. "I had casually tried to quit a bunch of times, and then 'seriously' some more times, but I never made the cut and I'd always go back," he says. "I would unplug my PC from my room, move it to another room with my monitors, and then put a laptop in its place. Then within two weeks, I would replug-in my PC and all of my monitors, and then proceed to binge on gaming for the next 10 days."[39]

Ending addiction is difficult, regardless of the addict's race, gender, or age. Scott is a forty-five-year-old computer programmer who became obsessed with multiplayer role-playing games like *World of Warcraft* and *Final Fantasy XI*. "Even when I wasn't gaming, I was thinking about gaming,"[40] he says. He began playing video games so much that his work suffered.

"I was falling down on my job," Scott admits. He neglected his marriage and son as well. After several years, he attempted to moderate his game play with the help of online support groups. "I'm going to try it again, but I'm not going back to that old craziness," he remembers telling himself. "It'll just be a little bit here and

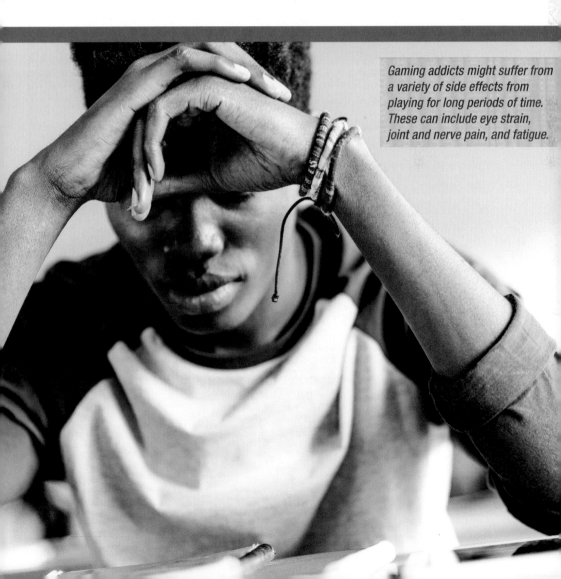

Gaming addicts might suffer from a variety of side effects from playing for long periods of time. These can include eye strain, joint and nerve pain, and fatigue.

there. I know now what it does to me. I know better than to get back into it." His plan failed. As soon as he began playing again, the addiction took over. Two years later, Scott sought help from a support group and with its help was able reclaim his life. "I'm very grateful to be mentally present when I'm with my son," he says, "and to not struggle with the feeling that he and video gaming are competing for my time."[41]

Dependence and Distress

The pathway to video game addiction is similar to the one that leads to controlled passion for gaming: the individual begins playing video games in childhood, makes video games the center of recreation with a group of real-life friends, and then branches out to playing multiplayer video games with fellow gamers around the world, often in marathon sessions lasting twenty-four hours or more. The line that separates an intense gamer from a video game addict is not always a clear one. Intense gamers and game addicts may replace other hobbies and forms of recreation with gaming; they may daydream about gaming when not playing, and they may conceal the activity when it meets with disapproval from parents, friends, and spouses. Both might also show signs of fatigue from loss of sleep, skip meals to keep playing, and even ignore personal hygiene.

The main difference is that gaming is a source of happiness for the healthy gamer but a cause of distress for the addict. The addicted gamer becomes alienated from other people, experiences anxiety because of gaming, becomes moody or depressed when unable to game, and becomes numb to the gaming experience itself. The addict may develop physical problems, including frequent headaches from long periods of eye strain and concentration, pain in joints and nerves from repetitive use of gaming controls, weight gain, and even a dependence on drugs. Despite these problems, they play on. They are addicted.

Chapter Four

How Does Video Game Addiction Affect People's Lives?

Video game addiction can take a terrible toll on an addict's life. A person who is addicted to video games often finds it hard to think about activities other than gaming. These obsessive thoughts can interfere with school or work performance, causing the addict to receive poor grades or be fired from a job. The increasing amounts of time the addict spends playing video games decreases the amount of time spent with friends and family and engaged with other activities. As a result the video game addict is increasingly isolated from people and becomes dependent on video games for feelings of self-worth. The isolation from others can lead to depression, anxiety, and suicidal thoughts. The depression, in turn, causes the addicted gamer to play even more, making the situation worse.

Portrait of a Video Game Addict

A forty-two-year-old recovering video game addict in the United Kingdom says that he was seven years old when he started playing video games. He was a "normal kid" who enjoyed school and playing outdoors. "Playing games at home was just a bit of fun," he says. But everything changed when he began to play multiplayer games on the Internet. "I was 21 and online gaming became everything to me," he remembers. He began playing *Counter-Strike*, a multiplayer first-person shooter video game, in which teams of terrorists try to commit an act of terror and counterterrorists try to stop them. The pressure to continue playing for long stretches at a time was immense, in large part because he did not want to let down his buddies on the team. But peer pressure was not the only thing that kept him playing. The game was a source of intense pleasure. "The rush I got when I got through to the next round, or made a perfect kill, is indescribable," the man says. "I'd physically tingle with pleasure and instantly crave that feeling again."[42]

Even though he was married and had a child, playing *Counter-Strike* consumed him. "I was happy playing my game," he says. "It was genuinely the only thing important to me. I couldn't live without it, and I didn't want to live without it." He began sleeping downstairs instead of in the upstairs bedroom with his wife because he wanted to play his game throughout the night. "I thought I was doing her a favour by not keeping her or our child awake," he recalls. "It pains me to say this now, but my wife and my child were a nuisance to me. It would annoy me if she tried to interrupt me playing."[43]

Everything that interrupted his game play was a nuisance to him—even his job. He worked as an assistant manager for a logistics company, a firm that helps businesses manage the flow of materials and products. He had his own office and computer, but instead of performing his duties, he played video games. He received three written warnings for failing to attend meetings, missing his productivity targets, and not making deadlines. Eventually, he was fired. "I don't blame them," he admits. "I wasn't productive in the slightest, and I had started to believe that going to work was great because it got me away from the arguments at home, and I was being paid to play."[44]

After the birth of his second child, the addicted gamer thought he would be able to stop playing video games. However, he explains how things became worse, not better:

> "I was happy playing my game. It was genuinely the only thing important to me. I couldn't live without it, and I didn't want to live without it."[43]
>
> —A recovering video game addict

42

Some addicts cannot resist the temptation to play video games at work. This leads to their work suffering, negative performance reviews, and even being fired.

The truth was that I didn't want to stop, and even having a baby in the house didn't stop me from continuing to play and introducing drugs into my day to day life. I started to use cocaine in order to keep myself awake at night, just to play for longer. As soon as it got to midnight UK-time, most people I played regularly with would head offline. But that didn't stop me, instead I just jumped onto another server to play with people in Australia or America. I didn't move away from the TV screen unless it was to go to the toilet. I remember only really eating takeaway pizza, if I ate at all. Personal hygiene wasn't something I even thought about anymore. I didn't help out with my young children. I separated myself from society but I was connected to people from all around the world. There was honestly no one more important to me than my online friends.[45]

Realizing that her husband put gaming ahead of their marriage and children, his wife asked him to move out. Their marriage was at an end. With no job, no money, and nowhere to go, the man moved in with his parents. But when his parents saw how much he played video games, they intervened. They forced him to go to a private addiction rehabilitation facility, where he received treatment. "It was an extremely difficult time, because I'd been addicted to online gaming for 18 years. But I had my moment of clarity and I knew I needed to stop," he says. "I'm not proud of what I've done, it cost me everything."[46]

A University Student Trapped by Video Game Addiction

Like many video game addicts, a university student who goes by the online name of AddictedDreamer started playing video games in childhood, at age eleven. His favorite game was *MapleStory*, which he played with a friend, usually at the friend's house. While he enjoyed gaming, he had a variety of interests. He studied the piano and played field hockey, soccer, and tennis. He had lots of friends as well. But everything changed when the teen got to high school. One by one he dropped his nongaming hobbies. "I didn't want to HAVE to go to practice when I could just play *Call of Duty* or *MapleStory* with my friends," he says. "Those were the first things I started giving up in order to play more games, the games I loved so much because they would constantly challenge me mentally."[47]

As is often the case with video game addiction, things took a turn for the worse when AddictedDreamer started playing a multiplayer online game. "Fast forward to the 3rd year of high school, a friend introduces the game *League of Legends* to me. The beginning of the end," he says. "Playing *League of Legends* was the world to me. It allowed me to do something competitively with friends, constantly get better at something and being able to show that I was better. It was the fun I got out of playing sports but permanently, without physical exhaustion."[48]

Video Game Play Causes the Death of Twelve People

Shortly before 7 a.m. on February 8, 2016, two commuter trains crashed head-on near the spa town of Bad Aibling in southern Germany. Twelve people died in the crash, and eighty-nine were injured. Officials estimate that the trains were traveling about 62 miles per hour (100 kph) at the moment of impact.

The accident was caused by a train dispatcher who mistakenly gave two trains traveling in opposite directions the approval to travel down the single track. Realizing his mistake, the dispatcher tried to warn the trains' drivers about the error, but he pressed the wrong button and sent the alert to another dispatcher. By the time he realized what he had done, it was too late.

The investigation into the crash revealed that the thirty-nine-year-old dispatcher had made the mistake because he was distracted. He had been playing the video game *Dragon Hunter 5* on his cell phone until just before the accident. He was charged with involuntary manslaughter and bodily harm for causing the accident and was found guilty. "His thoughts were fixated on this game," said Judge Erich Fuchs as he delivered the ruling at the state court. "He had no resources left over for operational procedures." The judge added that the dispatcher was not a bad person "but first and foremost became a victim of his own passion for games." The judge sentenced him to three-and-a-half years in prison for his actions.

Quoted in Associated Press, "Train Dispatcher in Germany Sentenced to 3.5 Years in Prison over Crash That Killed 12," Business Insider, December 5, 2016. www.businessinsider.com.

The teen gave up the remaining sports he played to concentrate on gaming. But it was not just his hobbies that dropped by the wayside—schoolwork did too. "I stopped doing any work for school, because it would give me more time to play," he says. "All I cared about was that game and getting better at it." Even grooming seemed like a waste of time to him. "Buying clothes, showering, using skin products or anything else appearance related didn't matter anymore to me, as it would take time I'd rather put into playing this game."[49]

Not surprisingly, AddictedDreamer's grades suffered, and this caused his parents to become concerned. "They had already read articles about how gaming ruined the lives of other people's children and got (rightfully) scared. This led to . . . a LOT of fights," he remembers. To avoid these confrontations, he began to lie about his activities—an important warning sign of possible addiction. "I got gaming bans, which I dodged by playing when my parents weren't home or when they were asleep," he says. He also was sent to an after-school program where he was forced to do his homework, but he dodged this as well "by always playing the friendly, down to earth kid, while straight up lying to their faces about the homework." The friction with the young gaming addict's parents took a toll on his relationship with them. "I hated my parents with a deep passionate hate because they were in my opinion the only thing between me achieving my goal,"[50] he says.

Parents can maintain some control over gaming when their kids live at home. However, once older children leave the home to attend college or move to homes of their own, they are unsupervised and gaming can get out of control.

Despite his falling grades, Addicted-Dreamer graduated from high school and enrolled in college. He lived at home the first year, where his parents still exerted some control over his gaming. "I managed to pass all my exams because my parents forced me to study and would straight up ban me from playing," he says. The next year, he moved into off-campus housing, with no one to control his behavior but himself. The young adult maintained balance in his life for a while, but the addiction soon took over. "Because my parents no longer supervised me my gaming shot up to a new level," he says. "I played and played whenever I could and I stopped going to my lectures and seminars altogether. I put my time into this game every waking hour and I stopped studying at all."[51]

AddictedDreamer lied to his parents about his poor grades, but they eventually learned the truth and told him that they would no longer pay for his education. This caused a crisis in his life, as he explains:

> I am on my own and I won't be able to afford my next year of university. This has forced me to only play more and more to escape the reality of all this and I feel like there is no way out. The only thing I can probably do is pass my next exams with very high grades and come back home begging for mercy but I only notice myself playing more and more, not being able to stop.[52]

AddictedDreamer posted his story on StopGaming, an on-line support group for video game addicts. He received several supportive comments and suggestions on how to quit gaming. Replying to the comments, he wrote that he had stopped playing

> "I played and played whenever I could and I stopped going to my lectures and seminars altogether. I put my time into this game every waking hour and I stopped studying at all."[51]
>
> —AddictedDreamer, university student and recovering video game addict

video games and was receiving support from real—not online—friends. "I have a good group of friends (all non gamers) I told that I quit gaming and they cheered me for it," he writes. "I also now have the social obligation (kind of) to not play because they will ask me about it."[53]

Physical Effects of Video Game Addiction

In addition to having devastating effects on relationships, school-work, professional responsibilities, and mental health, video game addiction can affect the addict's physical health. A 2017 survey of 24,800 US high school students by researchers at the Harvard T.H. Chan School of Public Health in Boston found that 20 percent of the respondents used gaming consoles and other screen devices (not counting television) more than five hours a day. Such heavy usage of digital devices was associated with daily consumption of sugary drinks, inadequate physical activity, and inadequate sleep. "Using smartphones, tablets, computers, and videogames is associated with several obesity risk factors,"[54] write the researchers.

Excessive video game playing can cause muscle and joint damage. In 2015 a twenty-nine-year-old California man visited the doctor, complaining that his thumb hurt and he was having trouble moving it. A scan of the thumb using magnetic resonance imaging revealed that the man had torn a tendon that helps move the thumb. The injury had to be repaired with surgery. When the doctor asked what he had done to injure his thumb, the man said he had been playing *Candy Crush Saga* on his smartphone all day, every day, for six to eight weeks. He played the game with his left hand while using his right hand to do other things. The young man claimed that he was not addicted to the colorful puzzle game, saying that "playing was a kind of secondary thing, but it was constantly on."[55]

Playing video games on a cell phone—using one thumb or two thumbs—has been found to contribute to other ailments as well. University researchers in Turkey found that repetitive actions

48

PlayerUnknown's Battlegrounds Claims a Real Life

PlayerUnknown's Battlegrounds (PUBG) is a multiplayer video game in which up to a hundred players are dropped onto an island and have to eliminate each other. Since its launch in 2017, *PUBG* has gained a huge global following. As of June 2018 it had more than 400 million downloads, including more than 200 million downloads to mobile devices.

As with other multiplayer games, the bonds that form among the players fighting a common enemy are great. A sixteen-year-old boy in Hyderabad, India, was so committed to his *PUBG* team that he ended his life rather than give up the game. On April 5, 2019, the boy's mother scolded the teen for wasting time online rather than studying for an exam. Shortly afterward the boy hanged himself from a ceiling fan in his home. Following his son's suicide, the boy's father has called on the national government to ban *PUBG*. Several cities in the westernmost Indian state of Gujarat have already banned the kill-or-be-killed game, saying that it was making gamers more violent and distracting students from their schoolwork.

A few months earlier, in December 2018, the Vellore Institute of Technology in southern India banned the game, stating that it "spoiled the entire atmosphere on the campus." Achyuta Rao, president of a children's advocacy group in Hyderabad, supports a nationwide ban on *PUBG*. "Children are addicted and it is causing psychological disturbances," Rao says. "Horrible images infiltrate their minds and cause adverse effects. Only a national ban will have a positive result."

Quoted in *Gulf News India*, "Boy Commits Suicide After Being Told to Stop PUBG; Father Wants the Online Game Banned," April 5, 2019. https://gulfnews.com.

on a cell phone enlarge the median nerve in the hand. This nerve enables the thumb, palm, and first three fingers to move. Enlargement of the median nerve causes pain in the thumb and decreases pinch strength and hand functions. Researchers in Korea discovered that excessive use of two thumbs on a cell phone—as is required in some cell phone video games—increases the angle at which the user holds his or her neck. This increased bending of the neck was shown to be a major factor in the occurrence of neck pain experienced by cell phone users.

An anonymous contributor to Game Quitters says that he is giving up video games not because of the effects of gaming on his employment or relationships, but because of its effects on his physical and mental health. "I'm already spending all my day at work in front of a computer, and I'm doing the same at home when I'm gaming," he states. "Every muscle in my body seems to be tense all the time, and I suffer from severe back pain." He finds it mentally draining to juggle gaming and his everyday life. "Constantly being mentally stimulated and stressed about making the most of every single minute of free time, thinking about gaming all the time, normal responsibilities as an adult, and everything else life requires became stressful," he admits. "Mentally I am a mess. Recently I started suffering from insomnia and panic at-

Excessive video game playing can cause muscle and joint damage. Some injuries can even be severe enough to require surgery.

tacks; I have more trouble concentrating, and feel like it's almost impossible for me to just relax. I feel irritable and depressed all the time and nothing about life seems fun or exciting anymore, even video games."[56]

Excessive video game playing can cause conflicts in the home, curtail the gamer's social life, negatively affect school-work or job performance, and even cause physical aches, pains, and injuries. Many people suffering from the negative effects of excessive gaming are able to cut back on their game play and restore balance to their lives. But others are not. They receive respect and accep-tance from other gamers that meet their emotional needs in a way that real relationships do not. Gaming addicts derive a sense of purpose from their gaming missions that is lacking in their ev-eryday lives. And the dopamine-fueled rush from playing video games satisfies their craving for feelings of pleasure. When they try to break away from video games on their own, many fail. And the destruction of their lives continues.

"I feel irritable and depressed all the time and nothing about life seems fun or exciting anymore, even video games."[56]

—An anonymous contributor at Game Quitters

Chapter Five

Overcoming a Video Game Addiction

Like other behavioral and substance addictions, video game addiction is treatable. Some gamers have successfully stopped playing by sheer willpower, but the failure rate of such attempts is high. The video game addict needs an organized, proven program to follow, one that includes emotional support on the journey to recovery. Although video game addiction has only been officially recognized as a disorder since 2018, recovering video game addicts and the parents of addicts have been forming online support groups for video game addiction since the early 2000s.

Since gamers spend a lot of their time on the Internet, online support groups have proved helpful to thousands who have needed help quitting. Other gamers need more than online support. They need face-to-face sessions with addiction counselors, psychiatric professionals, or groups of their peers. Some video game addicts need to leave their environment altogether to remove the temptation to return to gaming. For them, inpatient treatment at an addiction rehabilitation facility is best.

Treating Accompanying Conditions

Many video game addicts have a mental condition or disorder that accompanies the behavioral addiction. For example, research has shown that almost 40 percent of young adults with Internet gaming disorder also have ADHD. A 2017 study of 130,000 video gamers of all ages published in the *Journal of Health Psychology* found that gaming was the cause of 16 percent of obsessive-compulsive disorder issues reported among the survey participants. Anxiety disorders, mood disorders, behavioral disorders, autism spectrum disorder, and personality disorders are also common among video game addicts. In cases like these, both the addiction and the accompanying condition must be treated together. "Rates of depression, anxiety, ADHD are very high among this population," says Andrew Saxon, professor of psychiatry and behavioral science at the University of Washington in Seattle and chair of the APA's Council on Addiction Psychiatry. "If you can treat those, that might make it easier to treat the Internet gaming disorder."[57] Treatment of depression, anxiety, and ADHD usually involves the use of medications.

At the same time, many in the medical community are not convinced that video game addiction is real, since it has not been officially recognized as a disorder by the American Psychiatric Association. As a result some doctors will focus only on the underlying mental health issue. Cam Adair, himself a recovering video game addict who was diagnosed with depression, believes this is a mistake. "It's not as simple as just deal with anxiety and depression," he says. "They're all interlinked. Generally, what we find is if you're going to try to turn your life around, you're going to have to start with the gaming."[58]

Some video game addicts also begin to use addictive drugs such as cocaine and amphetamines in their quest to perform well during marathon gaming sessions. If the gamer has developed a substance addiction along with the behavioral addiction, it must be addressed and treated at the same time. Substance abuse treatment often requires inpatient treatment.

Twelve-Step Programs

Some organizations treat video game addiction using a twelve-step program similar to the one pioneered by the alcoholism treatment organization Alcoholics Anonymous. The success of the twelve-step approach in treating alcoholism has led others to adopt it for different addictions. Among the organizations treating addiction with this method are Narcotics Anonymous, Nicotine Anonymous, Overeaters Anonymous, and Gamblers Anonymous. Following the suicide of her son, Shawn, in 2002, Liz Woolley founded On-Line Gamers Anonymous (OLGA) to offer a twelve-step recovery program designed specifically for gaming addicts. Woolley's son struggled with video game addiction for several years. One day, when he did not respond to her phone calls, Woolley went to his apartment. She found Shawn dead of a self-inflicted gunshot wound. The multiplayer game *EverQuest* was still playing on the video screen in front of him. Woolley never learned whether Shawn had taken his life because of something that happened in the game or because of a relationship with another player, but she believes his video game addiction played a major role in his death. OLGA now has local chapters in twelve cities around the world. OLGA also offers online twelve-step meetings and online forums.

Moreover, twelve-step programs match each recovering addict with a person known as a sponsor. A sponsor is someone who helps the recovering addict through the twelve steps of the recovery program. Sponsors are not medical professionals—usually, they are in recovery themselves. They share their knowledge and advice with newcomers to the program and encourage them to attend support group meetings. The sponsor is also available around the clock to speak with the recovering addict any time that person is facing a crisis and considering going back to the addictive behavior. Sponsors do all of this while doing their best not to impose their personal beliefs on the people they support.

Inpatient Settings

Video game addicts who have tried and failed to stop gaming through outpatient counseling and twelve-step programs often need to put themselves into a new environment to disconnect from video games and, in some cases, all electronic media. This is where inpatient treatment centers come in. Such centers usu-

Some gaming addicts can quit on their own, but many need face-to-face sessions with an addiction counselor or other type of medical professional.

ally offer both group therapy and individual counseling. As in twelve-step programs, the presence of others who are struggling with the same problem makes the patient feel understood and supported. Because video game addiction has only recently been officially recognized as a disorder by the World Health Organization, there are few impatient treatment centers that are dedicated solely to treating video game addiction. As a result video game addicts often receive treatment at centers for other behavioral addictions, including gambling addiction and technology addiction.

Gamers in a residential setting undergo treatment away from their families, but the final stages of the treatment may involve family therapy. In this approach the therapist observes how video game addiction can be a symptom of dysfunction within a family, as well as identifying the family's patterns of interaction and how these fit with the gaming behavior. Then the therapist creates a plan for changing the interactions that maintain the problematic gaming behavior. The therapist works with family members to improve communication, identify and solve problems, and create a healthier, higher-functioning home environment. Including the family in the video game addict's recovery improves the likelihood that the treatment will be successful.

One of the few residential rehabilitation programs in the nation specializing in technology addiction, including video game addiction, is reSTART Life, which is located on a secluded ranch outside Seattle, Washington. Founded by Cosette Rae, a former software developer, reSTART Life provides a place for addicts to disconnect from the virtual world and deal with their addiction. The residents are required to eat healthy food, take part in an exercise program, and sleep regular hours. They are allowed to have cell phones, but they only use them to call, text, e-mail, and view maps. All other functions are disabled, and the phones are monitored to make sure that the user does not visit forbidden websites. The residents make a "bottom line" promise to give up video games or any other problem Internet content. If they have a drug or alcohol problem, they must commit to giving it up as well. "The drugs of old are now repackaged," says Rae, referring to technology. "We have a new foe."[59]

> "The drugs of old are now repackaged. We have a new foe."[59]
>
> —Cosette Rae, founder of reSTART Life, a residential treatment center

Outpatient Treatment

If an addicted gamer has a strong support system at home that will prevent the addict from accessing games, then he or she might not need to go to a residential center. Instead, the addict can receive treatment at a clinic or from a psychologist and then return home. This is known as outpatient treatment. Outpatient treatment offers many of the benefits of inpatient treatment, including group therapy and individual counseling, while allowing the patient to maintain a more normal daily routine. During outpatient treatment, the video game addict can receive addic-

The final stages of inpatient treatment may involve family therapy. The therapist works with the family to improve communication and create a better-functioning home environment.

tion treatment without having to take off from school or work for weeks at a time.

One of the most common treatments for video game addiction is cognitive behavioral therapy (CBT). Cognition is the process of thinking, and thinking is what CBT addresses. CBT begins by examining the patient's entire mental state, instead of focusing only on one disorder. After doing a psychological assessment, counselors help their patients learn new skills to deal with negative thinking. The patient is taught to identify the thought or thoughts that lead to the harmful behavior, which in this case is playing video games. When the patient recognizes such thoughts, he or she can then apply strategies to challenge and overcome the thoughts, thus preventing the harmful behavior. CBT has proved effective in treating major depressive disorder, anxiety disorders, eating disorders, and behavioral addictions. Research has shown

A Gamer Describes How He Kicked the Habit

A Seattle, Washington, gamer who calls himself McPhersonsw gave up video games on his own. He describes the process:

> The last six weeks have been the hardest weeks of my life. I forsook all comfort that I'd grown accustomed to. My home. My bed. A kitchen. A desk. A computer. Video games. And it has been the single greatest event of my life. . . .
>
> I made lists of what I wanted. What to do with my time. Identified the true nature and cause of my unhappiness. . . . I spent the next few days in a daze. I walked around Seattle for 17 miles on a Thursday afternoon. I had called in sick to work. . . . I went from sad to angry to happy to sad to angry and back and forth all over again.
>
> I did this for days. Work. Workout. Walk. Listen to music. Read. Write. Doodle. Every day. I read a book in four days. I wrote letters I didn't send. I screamed in my car. I drank more water. I took vitamins. I kept working out. I kept writing. I kept drawing. . . .
>
> I saw myself changing. I learned to stop negative thoughts before they became nightmares. I was more positive. I was happier. More confident. . . .
>
> I am proud. I am positive. And I am growing.

McPhersonsw, "The Story of How I Overcame My Video Game Addiction, and Realized That I Had One at All," Reddit, 2016. www.reddit.com.

that CBT can be delivered not only in face-to-face therapy sessions but also online.

Using Technology to Curb Gaming

Some people who play video games for long periods of time have taken control of their gaming by imposing limits on how long they can play during each video game session. Software programs, or apps, are available to automatically limit total screen time or the time spent playing a game. A recovering video game addict who goes by the online name of OneYearAtATime0 wrote his own program that would shut down his computer if he exceeded the time he set for himself. "With this 'gaming-clock' it was possible to moderate,"[60] he says.

A video game addict who wants help from a friend or family member to steer clear of video games can have that person download an app that will let them monitor the addict's activity. Apps like Qustodio, OurPact, and Screen Time allow friends and family to manage what kinds of content the addict is accessing and block them from video game apps and websites.

Finding Alternatives to Gaming

For video game addicts, gaming replaces all other leisure activities that they might have enjoyed before becoming obsessed with video games. As a result, when a gamer gives up video games, he or she will have a lot of free time. To avoid a relapse, the recovering video game addict is encouraged to fill the free time with other activities, either returning to old sports and hobbies or finding new ones. Research has shown that playing competitive sports, where the outcome is unknown and winning is strongly desired, can release dopamine into the system, creating feelings of pleasure in the participant. Intense exercise can release serotonin, another neurotransmitter that improves a person's mood. Smith & Jones Addiction Consultants located in the Netherlands tries to get video game addicts to see that they can achieve similar levels of excitement in the real world. To instill this belief, counselors takes gamers to a range of entertaining activities, including going to a club to go dancing, go-karting, and parachute jumping.

Replacing gaming with new interests is an important step for many recovering video game addicts. One hundred thirty days into his recovery, Slitz_Treaver, which is his online name, writes: "Ever since I stopped my addiction, I have been meditating every

morning, expand[ing] my social circle with people and being in tune with my friends' emotion. I listen more to my friends about their life and spend more time laughing with them. I also spend my time going out to live concerts, and I'm on my third book now."[61]

Since video game addiction is still a new disorder, scientists are unsure about the best treatment options. Adapting existing addiction treatment programs to this new form of addiction is logical, because all addictions share certain common features. But what seems to make sense and what is scientifically proven are two different things. Science requires that studies of treatment programs involve large enough numbers of people to accurately assess the value of treatment. The researchers also must track the participants over a significant period of time to see how many people remain in recovery and how many relapse. In addition the methods of treatment must be compared not only to each other, but also to people who received no treatment. "Definitive conclusions about the efficacy of any one approach or set of approaches or their comparative effectiveness cannot yet be made because of

Removing Video Game Temptations

Just as an alcoholic must remove alcohol from the home to have a successful recovery, and a drug addict must dispose of all substances and drug paraphernalia, a video game addict must get rid of things that would draw him or her back to gaming. An anonymous contributor at Game Quitters says he tried to quit on his own several times, but always returned to gaming. On his final attempt to give up video games, he made drastic changes to his computer equipment. He advises other gaming addicts to do the same and describes his own process:

> My parents and my online gaming friends all thought this was another futile attempt to quit—and any other time they would have been right—but this time I did something different: I disassembled my PC and sold my graphics card ASAP. Then I formatted all of my hard drives. This completely cut me off from going back, as the main games I was playing at the time were *PlayerUnknown's Battlegrounds* and *Rocket League*, both of which required a dedicated graphics card, or an amazing laptop, and now I had neither. . . .

> Build yourself up to sell your gaming paraphernalia. Disassemble your PC, and sell it if you don't need that processing power. Format your C drive. "Downgrade" to a laptop. If you're a console gamer sell all of it. Uninstall all your games.

Game Quitters, "I Tried (and Failed) to Quit Gaming Eight Times," August 11, 2018. https://gamequitters.com.

the lack of randomized, controlled research,"[62] states psychology professor Douglas A. Gentile.

Studies into video game addiction treatments may take years to complete. In the meantime those whose involvement with video games is ruining their lives have no choice but to turn to treatment programs that have proved effective for other addictions, such as twelve-step programs and inpatient and outpatient treatment programs that include group therapy, family therapy, and cognitive behavioral therapy. Now that video game addiction has been officially recognized by the World Health Organization, more resources are becoming available for both treatment and research. As a result video game addicts will receive more effective treatment options, and researchers will gain a greater understanding of the world's newest addiction.

Introduction: The Newest Addiction

1. Vishnu Gopinath, "How I Overcame Video Game Addiction & Reconnected with My Family," Quint, March 25, 2019. www .thequint.com.
2. Gopinath, "How I Overcame Video Game Addiction & Reconnected with My Family."
3. Gopinath, "How I Overcame Video Game Addiction & Reconnected with My Family."
4. Gopinath, "How I Overcame Video Game Addiction & Reconnected with My Family."
5. Gopinath, "How I Overcame Video Game Addiction & Reconnected with My Family."

Chapter One: What Is Video Game Addiction?

6. World Health Organization, "Gaming Disorder," September 2018. www.who.int.
7. World Health Organization, "Gaming Disorder."
8. Geir Scott Brunborg, Rune Aune Mentzoni, and Lars Roar Frøyland, "Is Video Gaming, or Video Game Addiction, Associated with Depression, Academic Achievement, Heavy Episodic Drinking, or Conduct Problems?," *Journal of Behavioral Addictions*, February 3, 2014. www.ncbi.nlm.nih.gov.
9. Quoted in Marley Ghizzone, "Q&A: Gaming Addiction: The Newest Mental Health Disorder," Infectious Diseases in Children, July 10, 2018. www.healio.com.
10. Cam Adair, "Breaking News: World Health Organization Confirms, Video Game Addiction Is REAL," LinkedIn, June 22, 2018. www.linkedin.com.
11. Anonymous, "Addicted to Gaming: I'm 30 Years Old and Still Living with My Parents," Game Quitters, August 26, 2018. https://gamequitters.com.

12. Anonymous, "Addicted to Gaming."

13. Anonymous, "Addicted to Gaming."

14. Anonymous, "Addicted to Gaming."

15. Quoted in Victor Tangermann, "Video Game Addiction Is Real and Professionals Aren't Prepared to Help," Futurism, September 12, 2018. https://futurism.com.

16. Patrick M. Markey and Christopher J. Ferguson, "Internet Gaming Addiction: Disorder or Moral Panic?," *American Journal of Psychiatry*, March 2017. https://ajp.psychiatryonline.org.

17. Douglas A. Gentile et al., "Internet Gaming Disorder in Children and Adolescents," *Pediatrics*, November 2017. https://pediatrics.aappublications.org.

18. Quoted in Jonna Lorenz, "Gaming Addiction 'a Serious Thing,' Says Game Quitters Founder Who Will Speak in Topeka," *Topeka (KS) Capital-Journal*, March 24, 2019. https://www.cjonline.com.

Chapter Two: Why Are Video Games So Addictive?

19. Quoted in Megan Teske, "Iowa State Research Shows That Some May Be at More Risk for Video Game Addiction," *Iowa State Daily*, November 6, 2018. www.iowastatedaily.com.

20. Cam Adair, "Cam's Story," Game Quitters, August 21, 2016. https://gamequitters.com.

21. David Zendle and Paul Cairns, "Video Game Loot Boxes Are Linked to Problem Gambling: Results of a Large-Scale Survey," *PLoS One*, November 21, 2018. www.ncbi.nlm.nih.gov.

22. Quoted in Makena Kelly, "How Loot Boxes Hooked Gamers and Left Regulators Spinning," Verge, February 19, 2019. www.theverge.com.

23. Quoted in Tae Kim, "State Legislators Call EA's Game a 'Star Wars–Themed Online Casino' Preying on Kids, Vow Action," CNBC, November 22, 2017. www.cnbc.com.

24. J.Y. Yen et al., "Association Between Internet Gaming Disorder and Adult Attention Deficit and Hyperactivity Disorder and Their Correlates: Impulsivity and Hostility," *Addictive Behaviors*, January 2017. www.ncbi.nlm.nih.gov.

25. Daria Kuss et al., "Neurobiological Correlates in Internet Gaming Disorder: A Systematic Literature Review," *Frontiers in Psychiatry*, May 8, 2018. www.ncbi.nlm.nih.gov.

26. Ninja (@Ninja), "Title Should Be 'Terrible Parents Don't Know How to Take Their Kids Gaming System Away,'" Twitter, November 28, 2018. https://twitter.com/Ninja/status/106787 7015213285378.

27. Quoted in Lorenz, "Gaming Addiction 'a Serious Thing,' Says Game Quitters Founder Who Will Speak in Topeka."

28. Quoted in Lorenz, "Gaming Addiction 'a Serious Thing,' Says Game Quitters Founder Who Will Speak in Topeka."

Chapter Three: How Do People Become Addicted to Video Games?

29. Quoted in J.J. Adams, "Is Video Game Addiction Real? Former Players, Statistics Say Yes," *Vancouver (BC) Sun*, December 14, 2018. https://vancouversun.com.

30. Gopinath, "How I Overcame Video Game Addiction & Reconnected with My Family."

31. Adair, "Cam's Story."

32. Adair, "Cam's Story."

33. Adair, "Cam's Story."

34. Adair, "Cam's Story."

35. Anonymous, "Gaming Addiction Is Real—Because of It I Lost My Family, My Job, and My Home," *Metro* (London), June 18, 2018. https://metro.co.uk.

36. Slitz_Treaver, "130+ Days and Counting. What I Have Achieved," Reddit, November 26, 2018. www.reddit.com.

37. Quoted in Rhian Lubin and Matthew Barbour, "'*Fortnite* Made Me a Suicidal Drug Addict': Dad Saves Son, 17, from Death

Plunge After He Gets Hooked on Video Game," *Daily Mirror* (London), July 31, 2018. www.mirror.co.uk.

38. Adair, "Cam's Story."

39. Game Quitters, "I Tried (and Failed) to Quit Gaming Eight Times," August 11, 2018. https://gamequitters.com.

40. Quoted in German Lopez, "Video Game Addiction Is Real, Rare, and Poorly Understood," Vox, December 6, 2018. www.vox.com.

41. Quoted in Lopez, "Video Game Addiction Is Real, Rare, and Poorly Understood."

Chapter Four: How Does Video Game Addiction Affect People's Lives?

42. Anonymous, "Gaming Addiction Is Real."

43. Anonymous, "Gaming Addiction Is Real."

44. Anonymous, "Gaming Addiction Is Real."

45. Anonymous, "Gaming Addiction Is Real."

46. Anonymous, "Gaming Addiction Is Real."

47. AddictedDreamer, "Gaming Has Been Ruining My Life for Almost a Decade. I Want to Stop and I'd Like to Share My Story," Reddit, April 17, 2018. www.reddit.com.

48. AddictedDreamer, "Gaming Has Been Ruining My Life for Almost a Decade."

49. AddictedDreamer, "Gaming Has Been Ruining My Life for Almost a Decade."

50. AddictedDreamer, "Gaming Has Been Ruining My Life for Almost a Decade."

51. AddictedDreamer, "Gaming Has Been Ruining My Life for Almost a Decade."

52. AddictedDreamer, "Gaming Has Been Ruining My Life for Almost a Decade."

53. AddictedDreamer, "Gaming Has Been Ruining My Life for Almost a Decade."

54. Erica Kenney and Steven Gortmaker, "United States Adolescents' Television, Computer, Videogame, Smartphone, and

Tablet Use: Associations with Sugary Drinks, Sleep, Physical Activity, and Obesity," *Journal of Pediatrics*, March 2017. www.ncbi.nlm.nih.gov.

55. Quoted in Rachael Rettner, "Candy Crush Is So Addictive That This Man Didn't Notice He Tore a Tendon," *Huffington Post*, April 13, 2015. www.huffpost.com.

56. Anonymous, "Gaming Is Killing My Mental Health," Game Quitters, March 10, 2019. https://gamequitters.com.

Chapter Five: Overcoming a Video Game Addiction

57. Quoted in Melissa Healy, "World Health Organization Says Video Game Addiction Is a Disease. Why American Psychiatrists Don't," *Los Angeles Times*, June 19, 2018. www.latimes.com.

58. Quoted in Lorenz, "Gaming Addiction 'a Serious Thing,' Says Game Quitters Founder Who Will Speak in Topeka."

59. Quoted in Associated Press, "'Tech Addicts' Seek Solace in 12 Steps and Rehab," *Tampa Bay Times* (St. Petersburg, FL), December 26, 2018. www.tampabay.com.

60. OneYearAtATime0, "I Spent My Whole Weekend Gaming and Then Realized I Had A Problem," Game Quitters, December 6, 2018. https://gamequitters.com.

61. Slitz_Treaver, "130+ Days and Counting."

62. Gentile et al., "Internet Gaming Disorder in Children and Adolescents."

Computer Gaming Addicts Anonymous (CGAA)

website: www.cgaa.info

The CGAA offers a twelve-step program to help addicted gamers recover. The organization has seventy-one chapters in the United States and another ten around the world. In addition to face-to-face support groups, the CGAA offers online meetings, a discussion forum, and a help line. Its website provides an online test for video game addiction and stories of gaming addiction on YouTube.

Game Quitters

website: https://gamequitters.com

Game Quitters is an online community for gamers who want to stop playing video games and get their lives back on track. Its website offers an online quiz to assess how serious a gamer's problem is and a step-by-step guide to help a gamer quit playing, as well as a separate guide for family members and friends of a gaming addict to help them recognize and stop video game addiction. The website also provides a forum, personal stories, videos, and more.

On-Line Gamers Anonymous (OLGA)

PO Box 67
Osceola, WI 54020
website: www.olganon.org

Founded in 2002, OLGA is a nonprofit organization that offers treatment programs for addicted gamers and their families. The organization has chapters in twelve cities around the world where gamers can receive face-to-face treatment. OLGA offers a twelve-step program for recovery but includes other tools as well. Its website features online chat rooms, forums, and meetings.

Reset Summer Camp
website: resetsummercamp.com

Reset Summer Camp is a residential four-week clinical program for gaming and technology addiction, hosted on college campuses in California, Texas, North Carolina, and Indiana. Reset provides a fun-filled summer camp atmosphere where teens are able to detox from their screen addiction and learn how to self-regulate. They also participate in individual and group therapy.

reSTART Life
website: www.netaddictionrecovery.com

reSTART Life offers both outpatient and inpatient treatment programs that specialize in problematic Internet, video game, and technology use. The organization works with individuals, couples, and families to better understand and address addiction, and to create an individualized plan to promote a healthy, balanced lifestyle.

For Further Research

Books

Pete Etchells, *Lost in a Good Game: Why We Play Video Games and What They Can Do for Us*. London: Icon, 2019.

P.J. Graham, *Video Game Addiction*. San Diego: ReferencePoint, 2019.

Byron Lonewolf, *Breaking the Video Game Addiction: Advice from a Former Gamer*. Bloomington, IN: WestBow, 2016.

David A. Olle and Jean Riescher Westcott, *Video Game Addiction*. Dulles, VA: Mercury Learning and Information, 2018.

Internet Sources

Anna Brown, "Younger Men Play Video Games, but So Do a Diverse Group of Other Americans," Pew Research Center, September 11, 2017. www.pewresearch.org.

Brian Feldman, "The Most Important Video Game on the Planet," *New York Magazine*, July 9, 2018. http://nymag.com.

Nathan Halverson, "Facebook Knowingly Duped Game-Playing Kids and Their Parents Out of Money," Reveal, January 24, 2019. www.revealnews.org.

Melissa Healy, "World Health Organization Says Video Game Addiction Is a Disease. Why American Psychiatrists Don't," *Los Angeles Times*, June 19, 2018. www.latimes.com.

Simon Parkin, "Has Dopamine Got Us Hooked on Tech?," *Guardian* (US edition), March 4, 2018. www.theguardian.com.

Andrew Perrin, "5 Facts About Americans and Video Games," Pew Research Center, September 17, 2018. www.pewresearch.org.

PsychGuides.com, "Video Game Addiction Symptoms, Causes, and Effects." www.psychguides.com.

Benjamin Pu, "What Are Loot Boxes? FTC Will Investigate $30B Video Game Industry," NBC News, November 28, 2018. www.nbcnews.com.

Victor Tangermann, "Video Game Addiction Is Real and Professionals Aren't Prepared to Help," Futurism, September 12, 2018. https://futurism.com.

Catherine Yang, "Why Video Games Are So Addictive," *Epoch Times* (New York), April 12, 2019. www.theepochtimes.com.

Picture Credits

Cover: iPandastudio/iStockphoto.com

6: sezer66/Shutterstock.com

11: welcomia/Shutterstock.com

14: SircPhoto/Shuttestock.com

16: Maury Aaseng

21: Andrii Vodolazhskyi/Shutterstock.com

27: decade3d-anatomy online/Shutterstock.com

28: Dejan Stanic Micko/Shutterstock.com

33: Shutterstock.com

37: Lenscap Photography/Shutterstock.com

39: LightField Studios/Shutterstock.com

43: Dragon Images/Shutterstock.com

46: Syda Productions/Shutterstock.com

50: Aaron Amat/Shutterstock.com

55: 4 PM production/Shutterstock.com

57: Elena Nichizhenova/Shutterstock.com

60: Monkey Business Images/Shutterstock.com

Bradley Steffens is a poet, a novelist, and an award-winning author of more than fifty nonfiction books for children and young adults.